Brilliant Diamond

A Triumphant Journey from Multiplicity to Oneness

Both your
Blessings on your
life's journey
Jenna Rai Miller
June 29, 2012

JENNA RAI MILLER

ISBN: 1466298499
ISBN 13: 9781466298491

Author Photograph by Karin Lewis-Cook

Dedicated to Jesus
I am grateful for Your friendship,
unfailing love, and forgiveness,
showing me the way, creating the journey in healing and
my return to "oneness."

Contents

Preface · vii

Part I: My Life · 1

Brilliant Diamond · · · · · · · · · · · · · · · · · · · 3

Earliest Memories · · · · · · · · · · · · · · · · · · · 5

Mommy Dearest · · · · · · · · · · · · · · · · · · · 7

Vacant Memories · · · · · · · · · · · · · · · · · · · 9

Searching for Help · · · · · · · · · · · · · · · · · · · 11

Dr. Bob and My Many Aspects · · · · · · · · · · 13

Elmcrest Women's Program · · · · · · · · · · · · 17

Susan · 19

Angie · 21

Michelle · 23

Journey to Wholeness · · · · · · · · · · · · · · · · 25

Reclaiming My Life · · · · · · · · · · · · · · · · · · 27

Part II: My Poetry · · · · · · · · · · · · · · · · · · · 31

Preface

Viewing mental illness through the paradigm of wellness, faith, and hope has inspired me to write this book on "multiplicity" or multiple personalities, known today as *dissociative identity disorder*. There is hope in recovery. I am a living testimony of that truth.

Born into a Jewish family, Jesus came to me when I was just three, six months after the sexual abuse began. I didn't know him by name but as my friend. If it weren't for Jesus, I would be dead. I tried to commit suicide at age eight, and I remember walking to school making up songs to Him and Mary, when pained and I felt like a motherless child. I had no exposure to Christianity. We weren't allowed to watch Christian shows and, of course, there was no discussion of this in my family. I walked out of the Jewish Temple when a guest Rabbi said, "There is no room in a Jew's heart for Jesus." Jesus was the mainstay throughout my life as I wandered, seeking religious emotional fulfillment.

I sought help when I was twelve years old by asking to see the school psychologist. I knew there was something definitely wrong, as my home life and school life were wrought with pain. I felt dirty and ashamed and believed that everybody could see this. I befriended adults in the school system—the office secretary, the nurse, teachers, guidance counselors—in hope that someone would recognize that this abuse was happening, but no one did. I didn't relate well with kids my own age. I was picked on, ostracized, and physically beat up.

Prior to 1990, I led a successful life. College was a struggle, being so ill, and there were times I couldn't move or get out of bed. I attained my Bachelor of Science degree, *cum laude*, in psychology from the University of Bridgeport and earned a Master of Science degree in counseling in spite of my own mental illness. After college, I became a psychotherapist in private practice while working in major corporations. I once received an "Employee of the Year" award and was gifted with a trip to the Bahamas.

Serving on the Connecticut Mental Health Counselors Association board during the late 1990s, I was the licensure training coordinator, and I set up workshops and study groups. I passed the National Counselors exam required by the State of Connecticut, on my first attempt, and received my license as a professional counselor. I referred my clients to other professional therapists after a few years and relinquished my license because I knew in my heart that I could no longer ethically practice.

In 1990, a psychiatrist was the first person to recognize that I might have multiple personalities, and I was thirty-seven before the condition was recognized by the medical profession. After 1990, I was hospitalized many times. One time, I was discharged from the hospital and found myself in India a week later. I went to India five times to spend time at an ashram as a refuge, following the teachings of the religious leader, Sathya Sai Baba. Sai Baba did not ask that we give up our own religious leanings and taught that God was love.

I have found that effectively treating dissociative identity disorder with medication may not be possible. Each personality presents with different symptoms. I was on so many medications that I became like a zombie; I fell and forgot to take medications at times, and it wasn't that I wanted to be "noncompliant." Even though I had a driving force within me to get well and heal from this hell, adherence was difficult.

Today, as a therapist I work with others who have dissociative identity disorder and have found some concurrence that medication does not always work. There is no one-size-fits-all approach. The dose needed for one personality is different from what is needed for another.

I believe that different personalities have different blood chemistries, which may make treating any medical ailment a challenge for the collective whole of that person. This is only my thinking on the matter, and I have no scientific evidence to back up my theory.

As a child, we experienced being robbed of control over our bodies and our lives. Having dissociative identity disorder is living with the terror and torment of losing control over what we are doing and who we are at any moment. It may be seconds, minutes, hours, days, weeks, months, or even years to come back to self, not knowing what occurred.

Mental Illness is not a death sentence but can be like walking a tightrope. On one side sometimes suicide beckons and to the other we are faced with challenges which create opportunities for growth and change. Life circumstances even abuse can be reframed as stepping stones which today lead to success. Resiliency, growth, and healing transformations sum up my life that stem from affirming, supportive, fruitful endeavors.

Part I: My Life

Contentment, and indeed usefulness, comes as the infallible result of great acceptance, great humilities—of not trying to conform to some dramatized version of ourselves.

—David Grayson

Forgiveness is the answer to the child's dream of a miracle by which what is broken is made whole again, what is soiled is again made clean.

—Dag Hammarskjold

Courage…is nothing less than the power to overcome danger, misfortune, fear, injustice, while continuing to affirm inwardly that life with all its sorrows, is good; that everything is meaningful, even if in a sense beyond our understanding; and that there is always tomorrow.

—Dorothy Thompson

There is no wilderness like a life without friends; friendship multiplies blessings and minimizes misfortunes; it is a unique remedy against adversity, and it soothes the soul.

—Baltasar Gracian

Brilliant Diamond

Special is the child, in her innocence and vulnerability, who creatively shatters into a many-faceted, brilliant diamond in order to survive an onslaught of abuse, whether it is sexual, physical, or emotional/psychological. The spirit is slain, and the pain creates many aspects (personalities) in order to survive.

I will share my story, my return to "wholeness," from a fragmented existence. At age two and a half, the sexual abuse began. Before that, I started to endure physical torture in the hands of a brother, who was jealous and wanted to destroy me from birth. I was too young to remember my brother's attacks on my being. However, my mother would recount stories with a smile on her face, laughing, almost gloating sickly, about his violence toward me. The body remembers the terror and pain on a cellular level.

Living with a mother with untreated bipolar disorder, a father who was a pedophile, and a brother who was sadistic was a terrifying nightmare. My family of origin established for me the severe trauma of violence and abuse that I manifested into many "aspects of self." I reference throughout this book the "family system" that consisted of over thirty separate identities. There were babies, toddlers, children, teenagers, males, and females, some hurtful and some suicidal. Most of those in my family system were young, according to those who knew me. People label me as a person living with multiple personalities or dissociative identity disorder.

Creatively splitting by dissociative methods was a means of survival. I healed myself of the many aspects of my being by finding out how each of them "served me" and embraced those that still existed, taking on the essence of their power as a gift. My journey in healing began by viewing myself as a beautiful, brilliant diamond, each aspect of self a perfect and pure facet that became stronger and more brilliant while embracing wholeness. I found oneness and became an integrated person.

Earliest Memories

While playing "London Bridge is Falling Down" underneath my father's knees, he trapped me between his legs and forced me to do sexual things to him. At that moment, this playful child experienced terror, never to be the same. He was so big, and I was so small. If this were an isolated incident, I might have been able to regroup and not been affected, but my dad began to require me to perform more sexual acts with him on an almost-daily basis. I learned that play equals danger and love equals pain.

I started to fragment, to dissociate from the atrocity I was experiencing. At first, I had no conscious awareness. As the abuse continued and he began using my body for his pleasure, I would focus on a tree I could see out the window of his bedroom and would float there. In essence, I left the room in spirit to survive.

My love and trust were violated, and my sense of control over my world disappeared. I believed that my dad loved me, that sex is what love was, and began to expect nothing else.

I know today that my father was very sick. He turned to me due to sexual rejection and absence of intimacy from my mother.

According to my father, my mother used sex as a weapon or a manipulative tool to get what she wanted.

My mom would send me to rub daddy's back, but it wasn't his back I was made to rub. At age four, I went to my mother and explained to her that rubbing daddy's back wasn't rubbing daddy's back, "he makes me touch him down there." My mom got hysterical and screamed, "What do you mean?" I repeated myself in the only words I had as a four-year-old. She yelled at me and sent me back to my father. He cornered me and said, "What are you trying to do? Cause trouble between your mother and me?" I'll never forget that moment, cornered between the dresser and the wall, when he sexually abused me again. My spirit was slain in that instant, and I collapsed to the floor like a wet noodle. My attempt to tell my mother was a cry that she would put an end to the horrific nightmare. I sought protection and action.

Mommy Dearest

When I think about the role of a mother, the words *loving, nurturing, caring, supportive, tenderness, affectionate* and *protective* come to mind. My mother didn't possess any of these attributes and was cold and barren. My mom did the best she could, but the stark reality was that I could not get my needs met from her.

My mom had no feeling in her hands and could touch a hot stove burner with no reaction. She burned me repeatedly and with excruciatingly hot water when bathed or washing my hair. When I was five, she took me to get my hair cut, and they were going to use a curling iron. I screamed when I heard the word *iron* and believed I was going to be burned yet again. I knew to expect being burned by my mother but from someone else, I couldn't bear the idea of pain. My mother grabbed me, threw me into the car, and beat me. On the way home, she stopped at a drugstore and bought a "hot cap permanent" to curl my hair. I was terrified of being burned, so when the car stopped, I jumped out and began to run away. My mother's legs were a lot longer than mine, so she caught up with me, dragged me home, and proceeded with the permanent.

Like my mother, I became immune to being burned. When I was in the second grade, the librarian carrying a boiling cup of tea was not looking where she was going and collided with me. The tea spilled down my chest. I was rushed to the nurse's office, but there was no burn or blistering, much too everyone's amazement. My mom was called, and I was taken to the doctor. He didn't find a trace of a burn on my body. I had already mastered extinguishing the feeling of being burned or reacting physically by dissociating.

There is no question in my mind that my mom was abused when she was growing up. Her mom died giving birth to her, and she was shipped from relative to relative to live until her dad remarried, many years later, to a business woman who also was cold and disinterested. My mom struggled with the absence of a mother or someone who could be a positive role model.

Vacant Memories

As an adult, I lost huge voids in time: hours, days, even weeks. Clothes, foods, and objects would magically appear or disappear. I had no recollection of how I ended up with new clothes of varying styles. Many clothes were not what I would select to wear or buy. Foods, remnants, wrappers, and boxes were the tell-tale signs that someone other than myself had been in my apartment. I found new books, makeup, jewelry, music, drawings, and writings that I did not recognize as my own. I did not know who I was or where things were and believed that someone was hiding things on me.

I drove each day from Woodbridge to Stamford, about a sixty-minute ride, completely without memory. I would remember getting into the car and come back to myself right before the exit in Stamford. This went on for years until I moved to Stamford for a brief period. At another time in my life, travelling from Norwalk to New Haven, five days a week by train, I got by okay. New Haven was the last stop in one direction, and sometimes I missed getting off the train in Norwalk on the way home. I became aware and present in Darien, Noroton Heights, or Stamford. Once I came back to myself and was in Port Chester, New York. It did get expensive having to pay additional train fares—thank God I didn't travel as far as New York City.

One time, being completely dissociated, my legs fell between the platform and the train. I came back to myself and began screaming in terror, fearing that I would be dragged and killed. I started crying out for help, while my body was slightly inside the train. No trainman was near. I dissociated again, and some gentleman pulled me into the train. I only saw the bottom of his pant leg, so I did not know what he looked like so I could thank him. I didn't know that the train couldn't move until all doors were closed. It must have been only several minutes, but it seemed like an eternity. I was hurt in the process and had to report to the Metro-North office in New Haven when I arrived. Just imagine trying to explain details of an incident you were not conscious of.

Searching for Help

I began to put two and two together. I was driven to get confirmation that I did indeed have multiple personality disorder, so my ingenious selves decided to take an evening college course at Fairfield University in Fairfield. The course addressed multiple personalities and was taught by a psychotherapist who specialized in this area. I heard her speak and silently cringed inside, while at the same time, I was relieved. She was describing my life. I was wearing my psychotherapist hat in that class and, week after week, brought in a case study detailing accounts of "my client." I affirmed that I was indeed dealing with someone who had multiple personalities. On the last night of the class, I went up to the professor and disclosed to her that I was the client I was describing. I asked her if she would consider being my therapist; at first, she was aghast but said that she would consider working with me. This therapeutic relationship didn't work out. She distrusted me and felt betrayed by my portrayal of my client in class. She also had lots of issues, and I didn't feel comfortable trusting her with the many aspects of myself, so she never witnessed my multiple personalities. I terminated our therapeutic relationship.

I then called thirty-nine different therapists, all of whom would not consider working with me. They didn't want to touch multiple personality disorder with a ten-foot pole. My anguish was excruciating. Finally, I called Dr. Bob in Bridgeport, and he agreed to take me on as a client. As we spoke, I felt a peace come over me. I travelled to see him, and within the first minutes of meeting him and being in his office, other aspects of self were present. He asked me where I had been and if I knew what I had done in the session. I did not have a clue. All I knew was that I felt comfortable with him and trusted him. Evidently, many members of my family system came through, from toddlers to young adults, each presenting completely differently, as Dr. Bob informed me. He had me do some psychological testing, and I'm not sure what it disclosed, but our journey together began, and my personalities were off to the races with him. He was kind, gentle, and very effective in the work we did together.

Dr. Bob and My Many Aspects

D r. Bob created a comfortable environment, a safe haven for my personalities to be present, and he gently brought me back into the room at the end of each session. Dr. Bob met more than twenty aspects of self in the time we were engaged in a therapeutic relationship.

In writing this, I realized that I lost years with just a sprinkling of memories and had been grieving that loss. I called Dr. Bob to set up a time to meet and help me fill in the gaps.

He was not able to find my records; they dated back to before 2000. Dr. Bob informed me that because my files were over ten years old, they had been shredded.

He did recall that I had lots of personalities that were young children. Evidently I had brought in crayons, markers, and coloring books, and my little ones were expressive and angry. He described my drawings as "ferocious." One of my aspects of self brought in a disturbing, angry monster mask that was cut out of paper.

Some aspects repeatedly uttered, "Bad boy, bad man." I have vague memories of "little ones" playing with toys on the floor.

Sometimes "little ones" were crying. There was a teenage personality that wanted to destroy me, and she put my arm into the fireplace in Dr. Bob's office. Thank God it was a cool flame, and I didn't get burned. Dr. Bob quickly pulled my arm from the fire and firmly scolded that aspect, and she never did that again.

Five-year-old Michelle presented herself in a Stop & Shop. She took over $100 of makeup, all of the same color, just with different pretty packaging. Michelle wanted to play dress up and was caught by the store's surveillance team. When the police were called in, there Michelle was, talking to the police officer, asking him all kinds of questions about his girlfriend and having a great time. The police called Dr. Bob when they had found his card in my purse. He confirmed that I had multiple personalities. Stop & Shop did not press charges, and the police drove Michelle home. I did not wear makeup at all, and if I did, I would have chosen an array of colors. Michelle was fixated on one color.

Seven-year-old Michael took a pair of socks from Bob's Stores. It was late November or early December, and he wanted socks to keep his feet warm. An angry, older aspect became present with the surveillance team and the police. They asked, "Did you take the socks?" This older aspect was so angry with the young ones, creating problems, that she wanted Michael punished. Bob's Stores pressed charges, and a court date was assigned.

The DA, my friend Susan, and seven-year-old Michael were present in court. The DA and Susan came up with a plan that I would give Michael a dollar a week allowance so that he could buy what he wanted. Michael was happy with that arrangement. The DA wished us all a Merry Christmas, and we were free to leave before the court session took place. Bob's Stores was not happy with the DA's arrangement and made us pay a $450 fee for the surveillance costs, equipment, and personnel. We agreed to pay it off in four months, though the managers wanted their money immediately.

My family system did journal for Dr. Bob, each aspect using a different font or changing the color of the messages. I was not computer savvy; the aspects had a better understanding of how to use a computer effectively and communicated with Dr. Bob extensively. I have no conscious memory of this but remember that my computer was left on and used in this manner.

Eventually, I ran from Dr. Bob, but not because of anything he did. I was terrified and could not accept that there were new aspects of self emerging rapidly in our work. I ended my treatment with him and am unaware if I ever said goodbye or explained my panicky feelings to him.

Elmcrest Women's Program

While I was seeing Dr. Bob, I attended a day program at Elmcrest Hospital in Portland. It was specifically for women who were living with multiple personality disorder. I really connected with a woman named Candace, who was the director of this program. My family system could come out comfortably, and Elmcrest provided a safe therapeutic milieu. I used to drive from Norwalk to a shopping center in Wallingford for the Elmcrest van to pick me up and take me to the hospital. I had no conscious memory of the drive. The only thing I remember is that my car battery was drained many times because I left the lights on in the parking lot and had to wait for a tow truck. I was frantic over this.

We had extensive group work. In one group, we gathered the women's artistic interpretations into a quilt made up of individual squares. The theme for this project was "Love Shouldn't Hurt." The quilt was hung at a conference, and it was fascinating to see all the different portrayals of blatant pain and betrayal.

My aspects dressed differently depending who was out in the morning in preparation for the day. The staff at Elmcrest had the ability to pick up on the patterns of dress, connect the dots, so to speak, and identify who was present.

I had little ones that ran away, and Candace would come find us. One time, she found us trying to take a fish from the goldfish pond. Candace gently instructed me to take her hand and walked me back into the house.

I had to be hospitalized many times due to multiple personality disorder, being at risk of hurting myself, and/or being suicidal.

The program was great. It provided therapeutic outlets such as playtime, group therapy, art therapy, and music therapy.

I believe I was at the Elmcrest Women's Program until they closed the doors. It was acquired from St. Francis Hospital, which had no vested interest in the program. I am grateful that my family system had this avenue available to them.

Susan

One of my closest friends, Susan, was a real trooper. She hung in there with us throughout the years of this ordeal. Susan received phone calls from many of my personalities—she said the seven-year-old would make the call and speak, and then a three-year-old would be present, followed by one of my ten-year-old aspects. Susan had conversations with my family system, almost nightly!

I often did not know who I was or how I ended up in different places. I had gone to see my medical doctor in Greenwich and dissociated upon leaving, driving farther and farther into oblivion. I remember being panicked, wanting to stop at several homes but being terrified to stop and ask someone how to get back to I-95. I asked for directions at a firehouse and proceeded to get lost because I couldn't process the instructions. Eventually, I ended up at a gas station (don't ask me where, I couldn't tell you). I asked if I could use the phone and put out an SOS to Susan. Susan came to the rescue. She remained calm and drove me directly to Norwalk Hospital Emergency Room so that I could be admitted to the Psychiatric Unit.

Once I was admitted to the Psychiatric Unit, I felt like I was being interrogated by the FBI. I had to repeat the mysterious "facts" at least five times. I guess they were not used to dealing with persons with multiple personalities and didn't trust my story, or maybe it was me who did not trust them or trust that I would be safe. I felt like a freak in a traveling circus show.

I had paranoid aspects that thought my food was being poisoned and my water contaminated, so Susan bought me a goldfish and said that if the fish could survive in the water, I could drink the water. Some of my younger aspects were feeding the fish, and when Susan returned a week later, she saw that the water in the fishbowl was almost black. The fish lived, much to her surprise. We cleaned the bowl, and she instructed my family system on how to feed and care for the fish appropriately. I had no memory of this until Susan shared this story with me recently. I always wondered what a fishbowl was doing in my kitchen cabinet.

Angie

My dear friend Angie went through the wringer with me. She is a good and faithful friend. Angie gave me Bible study classes in my home. Every week, she traveled to Norwalk where I lived, which was a good thirty-five-minute ride each way. I have little memory of her visits, and we both agree that I was overmedicated at that time. She was there at my baptism. I don't remember the event, but I have pictures, a video, and a baptismal certificate from 2001. Even though I don't remember that baptism, the Lord never forgot me. He was busy healing me and feeding my hunger for Him by His presence in my heart. In December 2005, I had a second baptism, and that time, I wrote a poem that I read at the service. I was completely aware and completely integrated. My baptism represented the reverent sanctification of being born anew in the grace of Christ Jesus.

In the years before my second baptism, Angie put up with my younger selves and paranoid selves that would call her, pleading that her son (who was a police officer) call the Norwalk police to stop what my alters perceived as threats to my life. Angie was extremely patient and tolerant while my different aspects engaged with a full range of emotions. I was withdrawn, quiet, scared, and isolated at that time.

During this period of "our" life, I do remember a young aspect that came out nightly, I believe, and made up and sang songs to soothe herself. I remember sitting in our large club chair and singing while being terrified and alone. I believed that danger lurked just beyond the front door.

Angie continued to support me. She sought different Christian resources and prayed with me, emphasizing God's promises. I found that forgiving others opened the door to my healing. Prayer and Christian fellowship are still important components of our relationship as friends today.

Michelle

Michelle was the licensed clinical social worker that I engaged in therapy with after Dr. Bob. She provided me a Christian-based, therapeutic relationship. My personalities were lovingly accepted, and expression was encouraged during our sessions. Michelle's office had many stuffed animals and some toys, which we all enjoyed. During our work together, I finally came to accept that I did indeed have multiple personality disorder and found peace within.

Michelle and I were asked by the psychiatrist at a local hospital to come to closure with our process so that I could receive services from a therapist that was part of the hospital's outpatient team. This psychiatrist did not favor my working with Michelle.

My aspects of self never felt safe again in a therapeutic relationship, so they went underground, so to speak. I was left to deal with my problems on my own.

Journey to Wholeness

Achieving acceptance in my work with Michelle was monumental in my healing process. I began having some conscious recall of the different aspects of self, and this enabled me to examine how those that remained were serving me. Once identifying how they served me, I embraced the attributes, taking on the essence of their power as a gift.

I embraced resilience, creativity, compassion, empathy, faith, hope, love, joy, and forgiveness. I also embraced a full range of emotions including pain, sadness, despair, guilt, shame, terror, fury, hate, grief, feeling suicidal, and feeling like the living dead. Revenge was a powerful desire. I came to a place of acceptance and did not judge an attribute or emotion as good or bad, it just was. I allowed myself to be at peace with my process. There have been many times of anxiety, but I view anxiety and excitement as part of the same energy continuum and prefer to hold onto the excitement of the experience. I do have choices, which is a new and powerful concept for me.

I found that I needed to embrace rather than try to get rid of the personalities; I knew this intuitively. It would be like a child who screamed and pulled on the bottom of her mom's apron to get her attention while the mom tries to push the child away. I knew that the child would continue to scream and escalate her attempts until she was given attention and her needs met.

Without forgiving myself and others, I was held hostage by my hate, terror, and pain. Self-loathing was very real for me, but forgiveness enabled wellness.

The key to my wellness was through acceptance and embracing the many aspects, finally relieving them of the responsibility of taking care of me. They were merely playing out the trauma of their experiences. Forgiveness freed me from a life of slavery to self. This culminated in "wholeness," "oneness," and becoming an integrated woman.

Reclaiming My Life

Asking for a new psychiatrist was the best thing I could have done. Our relationship has been respectful and dignified. I have been treated as a person not just a patient. He and I joked that I had a "designated safe driver," so I could relax about my driving with no memory and how I got from one place to another without having an accident. He began to titrate many of my medications, simplifying the complex "cocktail" I had been taking that made me like a zombie. He slowly removed the existing medications and replaced them with more-effective medications.

I integrated my many aspects of self and was now exhibiting symptoms of a person with schizoaffective disorder, a smattering of schizophrenia, and bipolar disorder. When I received this diagnosis, I had trouble accepting that I was a person with paranoid delusions and hallucinations. Lack of insight and awareness of my illness impeded acceptance of this current disorder. My last hospitalization was in March 2005, when I was in a fragile state. I have been stable since that hospitalization by the grace of God, the expertise of my psychiatrist, excellent therapists, and my commitment to take care of myself.

In 2006, I began reclaiming my life. I went to work for the first time since 2001. A friend from the women's group therapy I attended referred me to Richard Weingarten, Regional Director of Consumer Affairs with the Southwest Connecticut Mental Health Systems in Bridgeport. After a short time as an operator on the Soundview Warm Line, Richard asked me to be a peer engagement specialist at Bridgeport Hospital. I worked with the Geriatric and Acute/Substance Use units. I developed and ran seven different therapeutic groups to address the different populations. After a while, I was asked to train my replacement and was transferred to the seventh-floor psychiatric inpatient unit at Greater Bridgeport Community Mental Health Center. I also developed many groups for my peers, one being an herbal tea relaxation group. All my groups were well attended.

Between my peer positions in Bridgeport, I worked for different agencies, part time as a peer employment specialist and full time as a senior residential counselor.

In December 2006, I trained as a presenter for the National Alliance on Mental Illness In Our Own Voice (NAMI IOOV) program. I started presenting my story of recovery from my dark days to my successes, hopes, and dreams. In the spring of 2007, I was recommended for the position of Connecticut state trainer for the IOOV program, attended the trainer's training in St. Louis, and became certified.

The year 2009 was a turning point. With a strong faith and confidence, I truly reclaimed my life. I decided to have my license reinstated as a professional counselor. I took the thirty-two hours of continuing education units that were required by the State of Connecticut and submitted the necessary paper work in just over a month. As a licensed professional counselor, I volunteer my services to persons living with severe mental illness, serving people who have no insurance or not able to make copays, people who fall through the cracks of governmental agencies.

These last two and half years, I have worked with three women living with dissociative identity disorder. They are an inspiration to me, and assisting them has allowed me to be more vulnerable and connected to my own feelings and past. Our shared experiences shape our work together, and my clients say that they feel understood for the very first time. I am truly grateful to each of them. They are one reason that I wrote this book.

It is time for the stigma and shame of dissociative identity disorder to be eradicated.

Part II: My Poetry

Cringe · 33

Confused · 34

Candidly Speaking · 35

Oh Mama... · 36

Sharp Images · 37

Swirling... · 39

D-A-N-G-E-R · 40

Doubt · 42

Praise God · 43

Cringe

Wanting to die
Needing to cry
Keeping my head high
God knows I'm doing everything in my power to try.

Being in the presence of my dad
My past persistent abuser
Leaves me feeling isolated—sad
Knowing this is temporary, not my living future.

Still I cringe with disgust
He's violated my trust
He's so happy I'm spending time with him
So proud of me, supportive now…fast forward the film.

Painful memories
Fast fleeting stories
Scarred…
Wanting to take something sharp – cut.

Bleed out the poison
Of his acts of treason
My love for him has always remained true
His "loving" abuse was all I knew.

Feeling blue…

May 29, 2008

Confused

Feeling so sad...
Bottled up tears...
Afraid to give into the emotions
Even though they are so near.

So tired...
Heavy laden feelings...
Sleepless nights
Weary with fear.

Trying to be brave...
Trying to be strong...
Trying to look good...
So no one could detect something is wrong.

Struggling right now...
In this very moment
Anxiously sad
No feelings are dormant.

Help me dear God...
Hear my prayers for peace.
Help me dear God...
Move through this misery.

Painful withdrawal...
Feeling very unsafe
Trying to find that quiet still voice...
That will reassure this child she's going to be okay.

Uncertain...

May 11, 2008

Candidly Speaking

What's all tied up in fear?
Do I dare explore or go near...
So, so angry
I'm brought to tears.

Angry at the situation...
Angry at the lack of safety...
Angry at its meager dismissal...
Angry I could have been killed...

I don't like to own
Nor touch the anger
I'm so afraid
I won't regain my laughter.

Anger to me is a large black hole
That spirals me downward...
Downward into despair
Feelings that seem so bleak and alone...

God, please lift me up...
I've stumbled and fallen
I need you Lord now more than ever
Fearful I'm drowning in the raging river.

God, shine a light
Banish the darkness
Banish the fright
Respond to me lovingly.

Your child...

May 18, 2008

Oh Mama...

Your illness chastised me to the core.
The pain, torment, and paralyzing fear...left me listless,
dead.
Reneging on your role of wife and mother...burdened,
compromised me as a child.
Confusion roared...violation endured.

Growing up in such a sick household set the stage of a life
both baffled and stifled.
I had to respond to the never-ending urgencies of the
moment.
Living life wasn't an option for me.
Care-giving was the only reality.

Oh Mama, if you only knew how I hated you.
I am truly scared to own this truth.

January 15, 2009

Sharp Images

Just eight years old
Feeling totally isolated and alone
Painful existence
Both at school and at home...

No one to turn to
No safe place to go
My teacher this day said "hey fatty get on line."
The kids were so cruel.

I was beaten, pushed down into sticker bushes
Called names
Could not trust anyone
Painful, slain spirit...my heart bled.

Taking a broken piece of glass in hand
I wanted my life to end
I tried to cut my wrist
Something inside stopped me...even though the hurt was
excruciating.

I remember thinking...
Of this totally annihilating experience
Anguished...mental distress
I was wounded already beyond my ability to comprehend.

I couldn't inflict pain greater than the hurt I already felt
Cutting myself to end it all
Was beyond the scope...of what I could endure.
So a life of abuse...victim to the whim of others...is what
was in store.

Young though my innocence robbed
From the time I was in the cradle.
First my brother tried to gouge my eyes out and suffocate me
when I was a week old.
Violence endured...burned and neglected by my mother...
raped by my father.

Yes, sharp images plagued me.

January 30, 2009

Swirling...

Swirling images...colorful neither just black nor white.
Many, many choices...it's up to me to decide.
Faced with decisions...does one exclude the other?
I think not, however, I must weigh the benefits of energies
spent further.

Time commitments...
Does my heart speak to me?
I must follow the path before me.
Trusting, having faith that it is God opening doors.

I must not view life as a chore.
Loving myself and the person I've become...adore.
Pleasant is my present life.
Free of all past strife.

At times memories snatch me back...
The past is the past.
There is little I can do about that.
Cautiously I avoid that seductive trap.

Putting my little toe in the ocean of emotion...
I avoid the drunkenness of the painful potion.
Never forgetting, nor fleeing...
I allow myself an experience more freeing.

February 8, 2009

D-A-N-G-E-R

Who are you all masked up and garbed in mommy daddy
costumes?
Echoing in my head are images and words that send my
world spinning.
Tyrants...Rapist
Frauds a disgrace to the roles you chose.

What about the little girl you created...
She deserved to be loved and nourished.
Instead she was robbed of any dignity...unsafe, unprotected.
Abandoned by you...she was your prey.

Get away from me...
Get back...
Stay away, both of you like vultures.
You stole the "food" out of the mouth and body of babe.

D-A-N-G-E-R
No one come close to me.
I'm so scared!
The mere thought of closeness, creates anxiety.

Hidden well are my fears and anxiety...
Having to have it "all together"
So scared...so sad.
Diminished ability to cry...

Punished for the first sign of a tear...
I had to wear a smile...A dichotomy existed.

I had learned very young that reality
was threatening my will...
My internal essence of life and the will to live were
extinguished.

November 11, 2009

Doubt

When in doubt shout...
Shout so the whole world can hear
The pained and anguished child inside
Tears run like river rapids
Churned up by the rocks of life
Painful memories haunt vividly
So frightfully
It's hard to swallow
Choking on the words
How dare they come near?

Mother? Father? Brothers? Friends?
Take off your masks!
You are evil, hurtful, contentious people
Living in a world of pretend
So gullible a child
Innocent and pure
Squelched
Having to be strong
Having to smile
Living in the schism...torn and broken

Oh, mistakenly judging self...
there must be something wrong with me.

November 17, 2010

Praise God

Praise God from whom all blessings flow
His grace and mercy is what I know
His love and salvation are mine for His giving
It is with great awe I express my thanksgiving.

He has healed me...
My relationships are rich
Freedom from the bondage that once did exist
I feel great love for my family
where hatred did persist.

My heart is full of His love
My life is filled with His blessings
Before, I could not even imagine
That in my heart
I have forgiven even the most heinous transgressions.

Praise Him...Praise Him...Praise Him.

September 25, 2011

Made in the USA
Charleston, SC
02 November 2011